# РАСКАЗ ПРА ЛІЧБЫ

## THE NUMBER STORY

### SMALL BOOK ONE

ENGLISH - BELARUSIAN

*Numbers Teach Children*
*Their Number Names*

*written and illustrated by*

# MISS ANNA

Early Reader Edition of *The Number Story 1*
Bronze Medal Winner, 2016 Wishing Shelf Book Award

Library of Congress Control Number: 2018902040

Names: Miss Anna, author.
Title: Number story : numbers teach children their number names / Miss Anna.
Description: Portland, OR: Lumpy Publishing, 2018.
Identifiers: ISBN 978-0-9962164-3-2| LCCN 2018902040
Summary: The pictures and rhymes present stories which introduce numbers 0-10.
Subjects: LCSH Numeration—English--Belarusian--Pictorial works--Juvenile literature. | BISAC JUVENILE NONFICTION /
Languages: English--Belarusian
Classification: LCC QA141.3 .M57 2018 | DDC 513—dc23

Publisher: Lumpy Publishing
Website: www.missannabooks.com
Email: missanna@missannabooks.com

Paperback: ISBN 978-0-9962164-3-2
Printed in the U.S.A.    1 3 5 7 9 10 8 6 4 2

Хочаш ведаць назвы
Лічбаў?

It is very easy and a lot of fun!

Іх проста, весела вучыць!

Say-along our little jingle

Ты песеньку спявай-ка з намі!

starting from Number One!

Пачнём мы з нумара Адзін!

ONE looks like my one finger.

АДЗІН

падобная на палец.

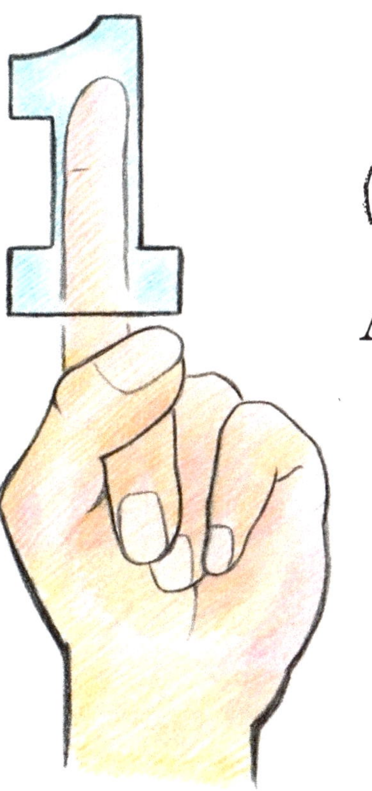

ONE!

АДЗІН!

# 2

TWO trails a tail.

ДВА

мае дзіўны хвост.

A TAIL! ХВОСТ!

THREE has bumps.

ТРЫ

выглядае як узгоркі.

Паглядзі на зялёныя ўзгоркі!

# 4

FOUR carries a sail.

## ЧАТЫРЫ

- гэта паруснік.

A SAIL!

Лодка з Парусам!

# 5

FIVE   is a racing track.

## ПЯЦЬ

- нібы гоначная траса.

VROOM
PPPPP!

SIX    curves like a snail.

# ШЭСЦЬ

скручана як смоўж.

A SNAIL! СМОЎЖ!

# 7

S E V E N has a sharp angle.

CEM

мае вельмі востры вугал.

BE CAREFUL! IT'S SHARP!

Асцярожна! Ён востры!

8

EIGHT   is rollercoaster rails.

ВОСЕМ

- як карусель.

ЮХУУУ!
YIPPEE!

NINE   is a bubble on a stick.

ДЗЕВЯЦЬ

- на палачцы пузырык.

A BUBBLE!
ПУЗЫР!

TEN   is an eye of a whale.

ДЗЕСЯЦЬ

- як вока ў кіта.

HELLO! ПРЫВІТАННЕ!

And I
0
ZERO   is an empty pail.

НУЛЬ

- гэта вядро пустое.

IT'S
EMPTY!
Яно пустое!

Thank you for playing with us today.

We had a lot of fun too!

Дзякуй, што пагуляў з намі сёння.

Нам таксама было вельмі весела!

We are your Number friends,
Zero to Ten,
Who will be here for you~
Мы твае сябры Лічбы
Ад Нуля да Дзесяці.
Мы заўсёды будзем разам з табой.


Bye-bye now!
See you again soon!
Да пабачэння!
Хутка ўбачымся зноў!

The Numbers are *SINGING* too!

To sing-a-long, look for Miss Anna Number Story
at your favorite music store like iTUNES.

MP3

Numbers 0-10
IDENTIFYING
& COUNTING

Numbers 11-20
& Ordinals

first, second, third...

Numbers 0-100
& Place Values

ones, tens, hundreds...

About Clocks
& Telling Time

hours, minutes, seconds

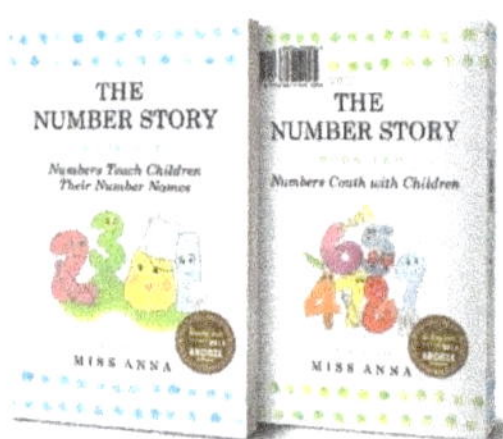

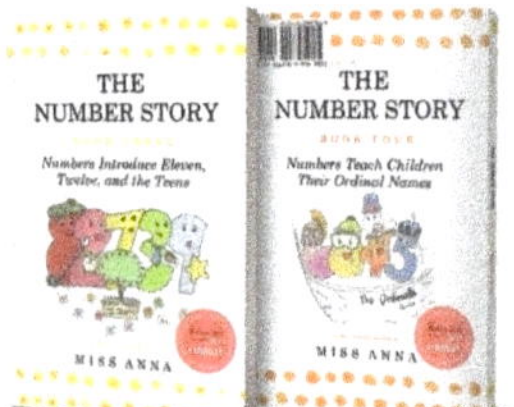

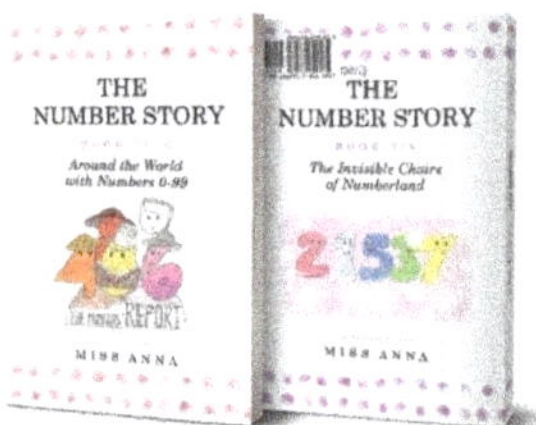

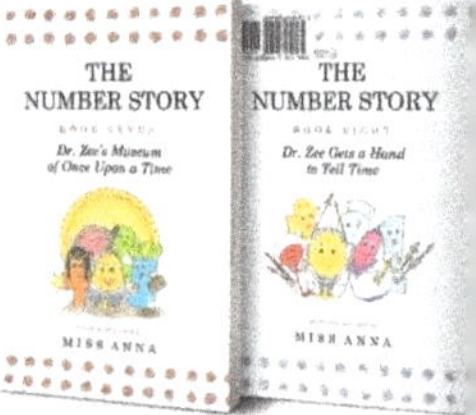

Number Story 1 & 2

isbn: 978-0-996216-48-7

Number Story 3 & 4

isbn: 978-1-945977-01-5

Number Story 5 & 6

isbn: 978-1-945977-06-0

Number Story 7 & 8

isbn: 978-1-949320-40-4

For more Miss Anna books to love,
visit us at

w w w . m i s s a n n a b o o k s . c o m

Numbers are working hard all over the world!
*Come Travel the World with Us!*